STYLE OVER SUBSTANCE

A CRITICAL ANALYSIS OF AN AFRICAN AMERICAN TEENAGE SUBCULTURE

Ron Mills
and Allen Huff

Chicago, Illinois

Front cover illustration by Tony Quaid

First Edition, First Printing

Special thanks goes out to the following individuals, without their help we would not have been able to finish: Ruby Hood, Yvonne Allen, Patricia Lacy, Don Freeman, Arlene Mills, Don See, Arkidia Huff, Rev. Ed.D. Leatrice J.W. Emeruwa, along with our family and friends.

Contents

INTRODUCTION

Scholars have studied African American youth and written books about them as if they were all the same. This is not true. They would have us believe that there is no hope or future for these young people. Statements such as "The youth are unproductive," "They can't learn," "They have behavioral problems," and "They display a lack of motivation," have been attached to our entire African American youth population. Although African American youth come in all sizes and shapes and from several subcultures, this is not how they are portrayed in the literature.

Style Over Substance examines one of the negative subcultures of African American youth. In this critical analysis, we look at several variables which distinguish this subculture. Then we describe practical solutions which have been applied in several African American communities in Cleveland, Ohio, to change this population's behaviors and thinking processes and improve the quality of life for the larger African American community.

This book is written for the scholar who wants to know more about this specific subculture. It is written for foster parents who find themselves raising an African American youth who is displaying some of these negative behaviors. It is written for one- or two-parent households who know that a problem exists but don't know what to do about it. Finally, this book is written for all members of the helping professions who work with African American youth.

The reader will not find pages and pages of statistical analysis. You will not find pages and pages of quotes from experts. You will find information gathered by two social workers who have a combined experience of 30 years working with all types of African American youth. We will share our strategies that have had a positive impact in meeting the needs of troubled youth.

The reader will not find a great deal of social work jargon in the following pages. We always wanted to write a book that everyone could understand and use. This is a practical handbook to be used by anyone who needs assistance understanding and working with African American youth who are displaying negative behaviors.

This book is written out of the love we have for them and the potential we see in all of our African American youth. This love and potential have opened our eyes, so we understand that our mission to assist these young people is much more important than our jobs.

Our book also tells the story of two social workers who went back to the community they were reared in to begin their professional careers. Even though our methods were neither understood nor respected by the colleges we attended, we committed ourselves to helping African American youth find their way in life. We listened to them and developed an understanding of the causes of their negative behaviors. Based on our insights, we designed programs to help them.

The original idea for this book was conceived by Ron Mills, who was later joined by Allen Huff. We have worked together for the past 15 years, and this book is an attempt to spread our philosophy, position, and mission to a larger audience who believes that all God's children can be helped.

PART I

STYLE

The Making of the Beast

The beast is the formation of a subculture whose values and norms are counterproductive to the success and survival of African Americans. Don Freeman is the editor of a community magazine entitled *Vibrations*. In his essay, "Authentic Community: The Crucible for People of African Descent in the United States of America," Freeman describes the beast as follows: "The contemporary values are materialism, hedonism, and egoism."[1]

The majority of African American teens have assumed a particular style of acting, behaving, and thinking. Many of our teens are more concerned about style than substance.

Style does not require them to process information because it is processed for them via TV, magazines, music videos, movies, rap stars, and peers. An example of this is teens shooting other teens for expensive sneakers.

Culture is defined as languages, beliefs, customs, tools, dwellings, works of art, etc. The family, church, school, and social agencies, etc., are the energizers for beliefs, values, and customs. They are, in fact, society's silhouettes which cast their spell on those they serve.

We define culture as the language, beliefs, customs, tools, dwellings, works of art, etc., of a people transmitted by social heredity. Culture is conveyed primarily by family, church, school, social service agencies, and neighborhoods, peer groups and media.

A subculture, then, is defined as a small group which temporarily rejects the language, beliefs, customs, and values of the larger culture because of simple or complex social variables. Subcultures will temporarily accept different languages, beliefs, customs, and values, or rebel against social variables. In this book, those newly accepted language, beliefs, customs, and values will be referred to as "components." These components are shared by peers via social interaction.

Components That Form a Culture

To incorporate style into a subculture, the following components must be accepted:

1. Music
2. Fashion
3. Values
4. Language
5. Recreational activities
6. Economics
7. Courting rituals

The ways in which the components are expressed will be radically different in a subculture.

One example of a subculture was the so-called hippie culture of the late 1960s. This subculture emerged out of White middle-class America.

The majority of White middle-class Americans aspired to live in a nuclear family setting, with the father as breadwinner, mother as homemaker and childcare provider, and children as silent, obedient offspring who wanted to grow up and be like their parents.

A minority of the teens from this White middle-class culture formed a hippie subculture. This hippie subculture accepted the following components:

1. Music: psychedelic or folkrock music

2. Fashion: long hair, tie-dyed clothes, sandals, and bell-bottom jeans

3. Values: "Do your own thing" anti-establishment morals and values

4. Language: slang such as "groovy" and "way out"

5. Recreational Activities: doing hallucinogenic drugs and marijuana

6. Economics: communal living, panhandling, street musicians

7. Courting Rituals: free love.

Today, most former hippies are part of the White middle-class American culture they rebelled against. As a matter of fact, the members of the hippie subculture are known to Americans today as the captains of big business and the inventors of "power lunches," "corporate takeovers," downsizing, and many other forms of capitalistic endeavors designed to hold their grip on middle-class culture forever.

As the popularity of the hippie subculture declined, so did psychedelic and folkrock music, hippie fashions, and language.

In other words, the components that defined the hippie subculture died with it.

Traditional African American culture is rooted deeply in extended family values. Several generations and families may live under one roof. Whoever is employed serves as breadwinner for the household. Every member available has a turn at caring for children and managing the home. Values are based on religious teachings, usually Christian.

Young people in the family are encouraged to achieve greater educational heights than their parents, and the elderly are respected. Any work is respectable as long as it is honest. Families have friendships that have lasted a lifetime.

Rich rhythmic music is an important part of Black culture, and its influence is felt throughout the world.

This new African American teen subculture has accepted the following components:

1. Music: hardcore lyrics, rap music

2. Fashion: expensive designer clothing is worn oversized and sagging below the hips. Expensive accessories include shoes, handbags, and jewelry. Fashionable hairstyles for males and females and expensive nail fashion designs for girls.

3. Values: "get mine," "get paid" hedonistic values. Things and products have greater value than people. Elders are not respected.

4. Language: a new Black inner-city slang has been accepted by the group.

5. Recreational Activities: the drugs used by the group are marijuana, 40-ounce and double deuce malt liquor. These drugs of choice can change at any time. They live to party.

6. Economics: one strategy for economic survival is the selling of drugs, such as crack cocaine. Also, the crimes of robbery and theft are used as economic means for survival by group members.

7. Courting Rituals: noncommitted sex, or, as this group puts it, "getting my funky off." The word "relationship" is often used, but there is little room for it in this hedonistic group. This results in a high rate of teen pregnancy.

Graffiti

We all understand that graffiti is a crime and an eyesore that needs to be removed as quickly as it appears. However, our attempts to study and understand this subculture has led us to the wealth of information contained on the walls of Black communities.

We examined graffiti from all over the city, mainly focusing on commonalities in the writings on the walls. In nearly all graffiti, there are nicknames and profanity. Nicknames are very important in teen culture. They are treated with all the importance of a title granted to a knight by a king. To put a nickname on a wall is to claim a piece of immortality. When teens write their nicknames on the wall, they perceive it as a living monument to their short lives. Mainly, graffiti is a cheap halfhearted attempt to grab fifteen minutes of fame.

We also studied a great deal of graffiti artwork. The

artwork expresses what cannot be put into words about the graffiti writing subculture. These modern day hieroglyphics express anger, violence, drug use, and self-hatred, and most of all, death of its members. The large number of graffiti wall epitaphs, such as "R.I.P." (Rest In Peace), are new to us. We never noticed them when we were teenagers growing up in the inner city. Such writing is clearly a unique product of today's African American teen subculture. Other signs, symbols, and messages found in graffiti are dollar signs, gang symbols, and the self-deprecating word "nigger" or "nigga." The walls of our city have a story to tell about our teenagers as surely as the walls inside the Egyptian pyramids or the caves of Europe have stories to tell about those ancient people. The story graffiti tells us about the subculture is disturbing. African American teens are clearly asking for help. They are out of control and in need of adult direction.

As the incidents of drug use and drug-related crimes increase in Black neighborhoods, the number of high school and college graduates decreases.

As the number of African American teens acquiring criminal records or becoming incarcerated increases, the number of employable African Americans decreases.

As the number of murders of African Americans increases due to Black-on-Black crime, the number of mourning families increases.

As the number of youth in this subculture increases, the impact of the old culture decreases and is less effective in imparting its traditional values to the next generation of adolescents.

With the introduction of rap music and music videos, this subculture has its origins rooted somewhere in the eighties.

A notable marker for its origins is the release of the first two rap records, "King Tim III (Personality Jock)" by the Fatback Band and "Rappers Delight" by the Sugar Hill Gang, both released in 1979. Music videos soon gained popularity alongside rap music.

Violence by African American teens also marked the origins of this subculture, as noted by Marlene Kim Connor in *What Is Cool? Understanding Black Manhood in America.*

> Cool had previously been a method of eventually avoiding violence; once accepted as cool, a young man was not challenged every minute of the day. However, beginning in the eighties, guns and violence took the place of attitude, style, and simply "proving" oneself. Cool was not being dictated solely by the boys on the block. With the advent of crack and the rise in popularity of rap music, organized crime began to prevail in a heretofore unheard-of way in the inner city.[2]

Even though an exact date cannot be pinpointed for the origin of this subculture, there are many markers dating its origins as the early '80s.

Media, especially music, is probably the strongest variable in the formation of this African American teen subculture.

African Americans are a very visual people. Eye-catching colors stimulate us. We like gold, not because it is expensive, but because of its color and eye-catching properties. We are fashion trendsetters; we will put on clothes with a certain color combination to catch the eye.

What has happened in the short span of two decades with visual technologies? Cable TV has entered almost every home at an affordable price. Satellites beam pictures of events from around the world as they unfold. Solid-state technologies have made television less expensive and have allowed television screens to be as large as a wall or as small as one's hand. Infomercials are half an hour long and music videos and shopping channels operate 24 hours a day. VCRs are attached to every television, along with video games that exhibit combat styles of mortal fighting to death, blood included. Specialized stores that rent videotapes and games are in every neighborhood. There are hundreds of new home video recorders, cameras, and printing technologies being introduced yearly.

These powerful new media aids help perpetuate the myths and stereotypes White America has created about African Americans, along with some of the myths and stereotypes we create about ourselves. According to the media, all African Americans talk slang, play basketball, gang-bang, pimp and prostitute themselves, sell and do drugs, rob stores, and sing, rap, and dance. African American teens are all school dropouts from broken homes.

If you doubt us, watch television or movies and you will find Black characters fitting one or more of these stereotypes on every show. The local TV news and newspapers help to perpetuate the myth that every Black male is or has the potential to be a criminal or violent. We challenge you to only listen to news on the radio. Look at your local news without sound and note that more visual cues are given to help viewers distinguish Black perpetrators of crimes. Most local newspapers operate in the same way. They spotlight Black crime by giving it much more space and pictures than other crimes. Little space is given to positive issues and accomplishments.

Rap music and music videos also perpetuate extremely negative images of African Americans. Why has this music become so instrumental in shaping African American teen subculture? There are two main reasons: Rap music is produced, written, and marketed to African American teens. No other music is as user-friendly for our children. It is no accident that rap artists speak and dress the same way; they wear the same hairstyles, use the same drugs, and could easily blend in to any inner-city Black neighborhood. Think about it, Snoop Doggy Dog, Dr. Dre, and other popular rap stars have an appearance that enables them to live in any rough housing project and survive. Their appearance suggests that they have done questionable things before achieving their fame and are still dangerous and very much a part of the African American teen subculture. The ganglike shooting deaths of 2 Pac and Notorious BIG prove that they were very much a part of this subculture.

In the late '70s, music videos became popular. These mini movies featured music stars performing songs in scripted situations. Music videos allowed viewers to see and hear the music. Almost overnight every song required a music video. MTV first aired in 1979, and even though it didn't play rap music videos at first, the music station was forced into adding them to its format. BET also gave time to rap videos, and for the first time, teens could see their stars performing their favorite songs. The singers and rap artists soon became role models to teens who were highly susceptible to visual stimuli.

What type of visual stimuli is given to African American teens via music videos?

We decided to answer this question by watching rap music videos for several days. We saw expensive cars, gold jewelry, car phones, pagers, and expensive designer fashions. We saw rap stars give the impression that they sold drugs or were in some kind of illegal trade. We saw alcohol, violence, sex, guns, and crimes flashed in these videos. We came to understand that any young African American youth who looked up to these rap stars without the ability to objectively process the visual stimuli might try to emulate what they saw.

Even more alarming than the visuals are the lyrics in many rap songs. Some of the most popular rap recordings contain explicit lyrics. These rap music recordings use explicit lyrics to describe sexual encounters, drive-by shootings, robberies, gang involvement, drug deals, and various criminal behaviors glamorizing the gangster lifestyle. In this way, African American artists perpetuate negative myths about African American culture that White audiences and our teens absorb. In truth, a small percentage of African Americans are involved in such negative, destructive behavior, but remember, the average American is media informed and educated.

We, the authors, are by no means condemning all rap music. As a matter of fact, we think the composition of rap music shows once again the power and genius of African Americans to reshape music we know, as we have done so many times in the past. Our major concern is the effect the negative images and themes will have on young minds which do not know how to properly process and filter information. As it has been stated before, we are the sum of our reactions to our experiences, and the way we react to our experiences depends on how we process the information and stimuli we receive. There is great power in the spoken word, and motivators, evangelists, politicians, announcers, orators, and actors all know this. We must respect that power enough to teach our children to process information rationally through their heads and not their hearts.

Eighteen years later (unlike the hippies), the subculture is flourishing and shows no signs of receding into the dominant culture. Strong and serious measures must be taken to help Black and young people so they can realize their full potential and greatness. This subculture exhibits none of the characteristics of our great and dignified race. We have survived many trials and hardships of our cruel history in America, but can we survive this subculture?

Simple or complex social variables can affect a subculture greatly. These variables can determine whether the conduct of a subculture is violent or peaceful, materialistic or thrifty, powerful or powerless. Social variables can also determine the longevity of a subculture.

For example, the subculture may fade into the main culture. It may be overtaken by the morals and values of the main culture and become what it sought not to be. Most members of the '60s hippie subculture are today the "capitalist pigs" they fought against. In effect, former hippies *are* the establishment.

As in every subculture, a series of unique variables comes into play to create it. These unique variables, combined with other variables at the right time, will help create a strong subculture.

An excellent example of a strong influencing variable was the Vietnam War and its effect on the '60s hippie subculture. The Vietnam War was a looming threat that young American men would be sent off to a faraway land to fight a war and be killed! This variable filled young White Americans with fear and uncertainty about their future at a time when developmentally, most young people feel immortal. The hippie subculture was a reaction to this fear and uncertainty. At the end of the Vietnam War, hippies became absorbed by White middle-class America. The key variable of the Vietnam War was gone, so the hippie subculture was free to become a part of the very establishment its members had fought against.

Social variables also have an influence on the conduct of the subculture they help to form. The influence of the war sparked widespread love and peace protests on college campuses.

On the other hand, the strong variable of racism has led African American teens to violence. We cannot have readers think that this subculture has been the only violent American subculture. In fact, the components of the African American teen subculture parallel the European American gangster subculture of the roaring 1920s.

Both cultural groups were fueled by the catalyst of the American dream that was stagnated by racism.

	African American Teen Subculture	**European American Gangster Subculture**
Music	hard-core rap	big band
Clothing	designer clothes	expensive pinstripe suits
Morals	get mine, get paid	get mine, get paid
Language	slang	slang
Drugs	crack	alcohol
Economics	selling drugs	selling alcohol and gambling

The 1920s gangster subculture was created by a minority of European American immigrants who felt that the only way to achieve the American Dream was to take it. They warred with rival immigrant gangs and the law enforcement organizations that would attempt to stop them. Lacking conscience or morals, they invented the "drive-by" shooting in their expensive cars, also called a "hit." Even though many of the members of the subculture were eventually subdued by the law, others legitimized their businesses and blended them into the majority culture in White America. Some prominent American families benefit from that gangster subculture today.

The European American gangster subculture parallels the African American teen subculture in many ways, but there are also many differences. The most significant difference is the impact of racism on African Americans. The bigotry experienced by European American immigrants cannot be compared to that suffered by African Americans since the beginning of slavery. European immigrants came to America of their own free will and were finally accepted by each other. Africans did not come to America of their own free will, and they have not been accepted. Some might argue that slavery and the physical oppression of Blacks are in the past, but we cannot deny the psychological effects of more than three hundred years of negative conditioning on Black America. This repeated negative conditioning is the foundation for the slave mentality of today's African Americans.

For example, the persistent use of the word "nigger" perpetuates the self-hatred that was born in slavery. Many young African Americans will use this word without a thought of its negative connotations. In an article in the *Cleveland Plain Dealer* entitled "The Forbidden Word," Veronica Webb says:

> Calling each other nigger as a term of affection or affiliation is a grass-roots kind of reverse psychology, where terms normally applied to our culture as a form of ridicule—terms such as "dope," "down," and "bad"—are used in a positive sense. . . . Traditionally, nigger has been a curse word. When Black kids call each other "a real nigger" or "my nigger," it means you walk a certain way. . . . You have your own culture that you invent, so you don't have to buy into the U.S. culture that you're not really a part of. It means we're special, we have our own language.[3]

The word "nigger" still has the strong negative connotations it always had, consciously and subconsciously, to African American teens. A clear example to support this statement is, if a White person calls an African American "nigger," this is not perceived as a term of affection. The word "nigger" is negative in its description of African Americans. Florence Scovel Shinn states in her book *The Power of the Spoken Word*, "Words and thoughts are a form of dynamite, and should be handled carefully with wisdom and understanding."[4]

The Bible says, "As a man thinketh so is he." A Black youth of the subculture thinks, "If I think I'm a nigger, then I am a nigger." And he will act like one.

Such negative thoughts may be the effects of racism and post-slavery effects filtered down through generations.

In *Chains and Images of Psychological Slavery,* Na'im Akbar says of slavery,

> The level of cruelty was incomparable to anything recorded in modern history, including the Nazi atrocities at Auschwitz which were fleeting and direct, destroying bodies, but essentially leaving the collective mind in tact. The protracted and intensive atrocities of slavery have had a lingering effect, and the pain of times past continues to call out from the genetic memories of those whose ancestors survived the test of slavery.[5]

We hope you have a better understanding of our youth's subculture and its style. In part two, we will attempt to describe over time when youth make these critical decisions.

PART II

DEVELOPMENT OVER TIME

We have spent many hours talking with African American teens about their values and views about time. We have determined that African American teens spend an inordinate amount of time in the present.

Development over Time

There are three time zones of thought: past, present, and future. A person's behavior and choices are greatly influenced by the thought time zone he/she focuses on most frequently. Also, an individual's thought time is influenced by one's developmental growth stage.

There are four developmental growth stages:

Stage A	1–13 years old (child)
Stage B	14–19 years old (youth)
Stage C	20–50 years old (adult)
Stage D	50–death (elder or senior)

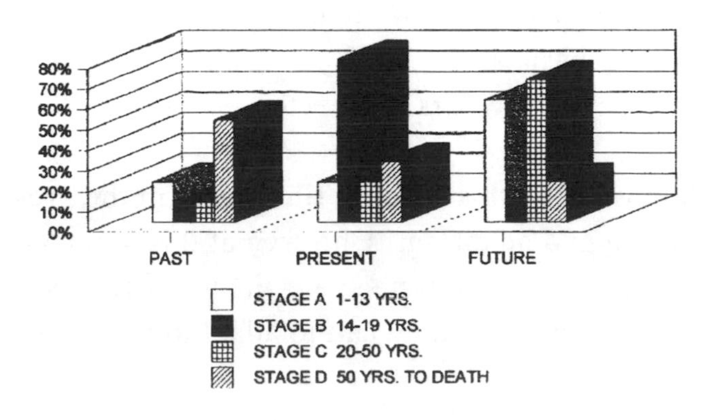

Developmental Growth Stage A

Children ages one to thirteen are in Developmental Growth Stage A. They will spend a great deal of their thoughts residing in the *future* time zone of thought. As a matter of fact, in Growth Stage A, 60 percent of a child's idea of the future is as a teenager. Children at this stage want nothing more than to become big girls and boys (teenagers). They look up to older children and want to have the semi-freedom and social lives of teenagers. In short, these elementary children want to be adults in the bodies of teenagers. They want the privilege of adult mobility, but none of the responsibilities. At this stage, children perceive those in their mid-twenties and older as old and boring. In Stage A, about 20 percent of a child's thoughts reside in the *past* time zone. At this stage of development, past lessons are used to recall survival and coping techniques for the present. The following are examples of helpful recalled lessons:

- fire is hot
- potty training
- how to dress
- ABC's, counting, etc.
- basic social skills
- days, colors, time, etc.

Almost all of this thought time spent in the present is spent learning and adapting. Children at this stage are fantastic learners. The little time spent in the present is mainly dedicated to learning all they can to adapt to their surroundings.

Developmental Growth Stage B

In Developmental Growth Stage B, youth's ages range from 14 to 19 years old. Eighty percent of their thoughts focus on immediate gratification in the present. The child's thoughts may reside in such a great percentage of the present that these thoughts may distort reality, making the youth very vulnerable to many negative influences or a style mentality that may lead to the formation of the teen subculture. At this stage of development, youth do not produce or create anything, but they consume time, recreational pleasures, material goods, sensual pleasures, space, and even relationships in a hedonistic frenzy.

It is at this stage that young people desert their family traditions with reckless abandon. Religion, personal conduct, sexual behavior, dress, and language are often toppled by the influences of the mainstream culture, i.e., popular media and big business. Youth will spend an excessive amount of money for the right type of jeans, sweater, or gym shoes.

At this impressionable stage the drug culture can become attractive. Gang life is poised to replace home and church life.

About 10 percent of a child's thoughts are focused in the future in Developmental Growth Stage B. These thoughts of the future may be fear induced or forced by a parent, caretaker, or counselor. Some of these future thoughts may not be realistic.

A key example of fear inducing thoughts comes from our years as social workers serving African American teenagers. We facilitate teen groups and in our sessions often try to get participants to link their present school studies and performance with their future career desires. Youth would look at their poor grades and attitude marks and would say how they wanted to go to college and play basketball or football. Many of our group members did not have the grades to allow them to even play high school sports. Sadly, when we bring up the topic it's usually the first time these youth hear that their fantasized future was just that, a fantasy. Many times we found that we were the first adults to ask them this question. The group participants then would respond out of fear of the future. The present was comfortable, safe, and not foreign to our group participants.

Finally, in Developmental Growth Stage B, young people's thoughts reside in the past about 10 percent of the time. These thoughts consist of lessons learned that help the youth cater to his desires in the present. There is some sentimental value of memories at this stage, but not much.

Developmental Growth Stage C

In this growth stage, the ages range from 20 to 50 years. Adults spend most of their lives thinking about the future. Adults at this stage focus their thoughts on future careers and personal goals. As adults become parents, they spend a great deal of thought on their family's future.

Examples:

Future Family—Looking for the perfect mate
Future Shelter—Buying a home
Future Security—Investing, careers, pensions, life insurance, etc.
Future of Child—Securing funds for private school and college.

The problem with this stage of development is that adults may spend such a large percentage of thought time in the future that important emotional and spiritual issues of the present may be overlooked, unrecognized, or unattended to.

At Stage C, 20 percent of adult thought time is in the present, specifically, maintaining or upgrading their lives and standard of living. Lastly, at Stage C, about 10 percent of adult time is spent in thinking about the past. At this stage, adults will have developed a more complex form of reminiscing about the past. These thoughts include memories of places, music, smells, emotions, and architecture. The past is used for pleasure as well as a tool during this stage. We remember the good times and we learn from our mistakes.

Developmental Growth Stage D

In this stage of development, ages range from 51 years to death. Elders spend about 50 percent of their time in past time thought, focusing on time lost, unhappy memories, regrets, and second-guessing about what could have been. They also think about happy times and events, people, special places, and important wisdom gained.

At Stage D, 30 percent of the elder's thinking is spent in the present to maintain the quality of life, including family and community ties. Elders also spend much present time thought focusing on health issues because their bodies are showing the wear and tear of age.

Lastly, 20 percent of our elder's time thought is spent in the future. Elders are concerned about leaving their legacy to future generations. They also think about the afterlife and what awaits them there. This is why many elders often turn to the church to ease the fear of death.

Returning to our target population, youth between the ages of 14 and 19, our concern is the excessive amount of time spent in the present to the detriment of the future and the little appreciation of the past. This may explain why many youth are not acting like adults when they reach their twenties. It may also explain why many are unable to live independent of their parents. We have noticed the conversation between youth and young adults is very similar. Many only talk about materialism, music, hair, and sex.

In part three, we must provide our youth with substance and encourage them to prepare for the future.

DEVELOPMENTAL TIME THOUGHT GRAPHS

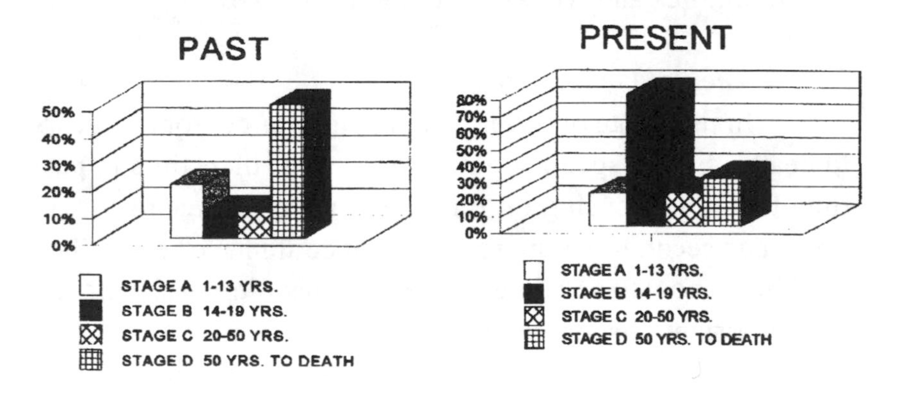

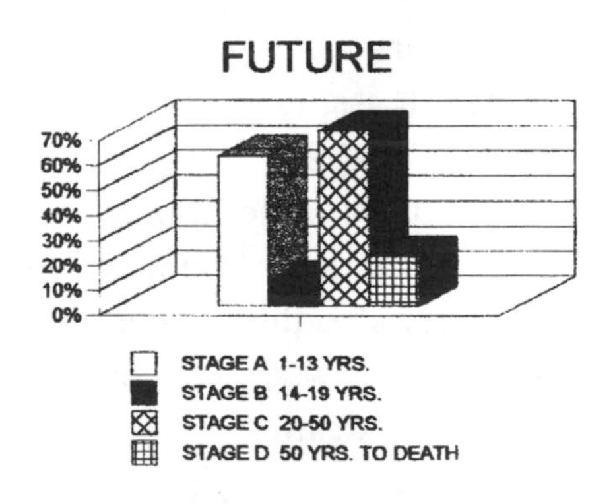

PART III

SUBSTANCE

Substance

Thus far we have focused a great deal of our argument on identifying and outlining the conditions which assist in forming a negative African American teenage subculture. In Part Three we will illustrate how African American parents, community-based organizations, and the African American community itself can have a positive impact on this counter-productive subculture.

We will reinforce our concepts by discussing several models that have been developed and implemented by the authors and other African American service providers. These approaches have produced positive results with the subculture.

What is "substance" and why is it so important in the development of a young person? According to Webster, substance is "essential character or essence. The most basic or important quality or part."[6] Substance is the essential character of a person that reacts positively or negatively to the environment and experiences. In this section, we'll examine ways in which to bring out the essential character of young people—that part that will enable them to process information and react to their environment in a positive manner. Only then will they be able to identify and pursue life aspirations and goals.

A substance mentality is developed in African American children through early informal education, formal education, training, planning, exposure, and most of all, adult involvement. In short, a substance mentality led to the continuous struggle for freedom by African Americans. It is this substance mentality which provides a sense of hope and vision that drives African Americans forward against all odds.

How is it that two African American children can grow up in the same economically disadvantaged inner-city housing project, yet turn out completely different? One becomes a drug dealer, the other a social worker or a doctor. Substance makes the true man or woman. Substance is permanent and resides deep in one's soul; style is superficial, temporary, and can be changed and copied.

Parents/Guardians/Caregivers

Building substance is an ongoing process. At each stage of development, a person has the opportunity to build character. How we process experiences and information determines the content of our character. These substances are acquired through processing information. Parents (our first teachers) teach us how to interpret and process information. Sultan Adul Latif and Namah Latif, in their book *Slavery: The African-American Psychic Trauma*, state, "A parent's most important job is to prepare the child for a responsible adulthood. This cannot be done if the parent has an 'I don't want to be bothered,' attitude."[7]

Black parents are all-important in this character-building process. Through parents, children learn to decipher their childhood experiences, as well as how to react to the experiences. To understand this process fully, we can compare the parent or caretaker to soil and the child to the growing tree. As the soil, parents contain the nutrients to help the child grow and thrive. As the soil, parents are the first firm foundation upon which their children stand. As the soil, parents provide the fertilizer for the child's emotional and physical development. The parental contact is direct and constant. In a healthy family, the parent will provide strong roots that will hold and sustain the child throughout his life.

Parents and Family

There is an old African proverb that says that "The ruin of a nation begins in the home of its people." African American parents must construct the armor for Black children to wear in their fight against negative peer pressure. Parents must prepare Black children to leave the nest by helping them acquire the necessary skills to survive and thrive in American society. Many African American families have destroyed their greatest asset by choosing to accept the American middle-class concept of the nuclear family. Our African heritage is one that strongly embraces the extended family concept. It clearly was the reason for our past child-rearing successes. Grandparents provide a wealth of parenting knowledge and skill. Grandfathers, uncles, and cousins served as role models for male children. These extended family units worked as mini villages to raise children.

The nuclear Black family has left many Black families isolated and without the powerful support needed to sustain them in these difficult times.

To be a strong family unit, parents' expectations must be high and must be matched by parental actions. Parents must guard against sending their children mixed messages. As social workers assigned to do outreach in an inner-city community with African American youth, we can recall countless times when parents expressed their concerns with their children's lack of interest in school and their unwillingness to perform academically, but these children's rooms were always furnished with televisions, stereos, VCRs, video games, and compact disk players. We have never found a desk or study center equipped with adequate materials, such as reference books, computers, encyclopedia, maps, etc., necessary to complete school assignments or homework. These parents literally go into debt buying recreational and leisure products, but seldom do they spend money on materials that deal with education. Consequently, their children place a lower priority on education.

Such behavior can be perceived as a parent inadvertently rewarding failure. African American parents will spend many dollars on expensive clothing for children, but they will not match or exceed this spending in educational pursuits. Inner-city high schools have almost a 50 percent dropout rate. Yet according to research done by *Advertising Age*, African Americans will spend more money than Anglos, Hispanics, and Asians on clothing.

African Americans frequent department stores and product specialty stores more than other ethnic groups, and dime stores less than other ethnic groups. We hardly think that any teen with failing grades merits expensive brand name sneakers, jeans, or Starter jackets. This behavior on the part of parents does not promote a good work ethic, but it does reward failure. The priority must be placed on teaching the child to value education.

Parents and family are the primary teachers of African American children, and their expectations for personal conduct must also be high. African American children must be taught that they represent their family and community. Their family's name must be something special, and they should think of themselves as ambassadors. Families should teach their children family history as well as African American history. Family history should focus on some of the following facts:

- The first family member to come to America (if possible)

- The first family member to migrate north
- The oldest living patriarch of the family
- The oldest living matriarch of the family
- The first family member to receive a college degree
- Landowners in the family
- The talents and skills of family members
- A family tree.

The purpose of these activities is to instill family and racial pride and honor. We must inform African American youth that our ancestors braved several generations of slavery and torment with hopes that some future descendant would live as a free person. We all are those future descendants and we must not engage in criminal behaviors that would jeopardize that freedom. The bravery, determination, and courage of our enslaved African ancestors must not go in vain. The most important thing a family can and must do is to build substance over style.

This essential character is what Martin Luther King Jr. had in mind when he stated, "A man should not be judged on the color of his skin, but on the content of his character."

African American parents must help children to decode information about their history and culture. They must teach them how to communicate and establish a positive sense of self, of who they are in a world that defines them in negative terms. African American parents must help children to understand their uniqueness. They must share with them the fact that they were placed on this planet with special gifts to share with all of mankind. Parents must begin to teach their children that they are precious. They must help them process information about their history and culture. They must teach them how to communicate and establish a sense of self, who they are, their uniqueness, and self-worth. These are the keys to help children celebrate who they are.

Sultan and Naimah Latif state,

> "A child may be raised by loving, patient parents, yet because of repeated psychological assaults from a racist society, may still end up an emotionally scarred adult. This is where creating a positive, cultural identity is important. Parents cannot leave such things to chance. Failure to instill pride in an African heritage will result in the child first becoming confused and finally feeling inferior.[8]"

If Black parents do a good job during this developmental stage, African American children will know that they come from a great heritage and that they are special. Also, a child will be less likely to value style over substance because he will have a positive outlook on life.

During the latter part of this stage, the child-parent relationship will experience a series of crises and challenges. This is normal. The child's needs, wants, and world will expand. At this point, the African American parent must continue to provide consistent direction to assist the child to the next stage. It is during this period that Marquits Hill's book, *Training African-American Parents for Success: An Afrocentric Parenting Guide*, becomes valuable. She says that

> During this period (pre-adolescent) it is important for parents to get their children involved in healthy and positive activities, particularly in the community that they live in, as children at this stage are easily influenced by their peers.

> Parent involvement is more and more critical during this age range because children are subject to real peer pressure, pressure from the media to grow and develop more rapidly, pressure from school to succeed and from commercial advantages/disadvantages of parents trying to give their children the edge or give their children what they did not have.
>
> Parents should be leery of doing that because children are left with no childhood of their own as they live through their parents' second childhood. Also, they do not understand the moral implications of having everything given to them as opposed to learning how to earn things for themselves.[9]

We recommend that parents establish a specific time during the day or evening (preferably after school) when they can sit down and communicate with their children. This time should be mutually agreed upon by all parties. If you can't get the child to agree, then go ahead and establish the time. Remember, you are still the parent. You are in control. This time should be used to discuss the following:

- extracurricular activities
- sexuality
- academic performance
- expectations
- school behavior
- dress
- school attendance
- culture and history

- peers
- career aspirations
- areas of interest
- alcohol/drugs
- or anything else either one of you needs to discuss.

We recommend that you help your children gain perspective and set goals. Help them to see that there is life after the teenage years. Give them hope so that they can create a vision for tomorrow. This will not happen if you do not plan for it to happen.

Through these daily talks, you will be teaching your children to communicate. How they communicate and interpret these issues to themselves and others is very important in their character development. Particular attention should center around the following topics:

Personal development
Goal setting
African and African American history and culture
Human sexuality
Technological changes

Always be mindful of providing information that is age appropriate. The issues mentioned above confront your child outside the home on a daily basis. At this stage, the parent still must continue to give the child hands-on supervision to ensure the full development of the primary skills needed to adapt to the outside environment.

We have observed that it is during latter years of Stage A (1–13 years) when children begin to encounter more of the outside world without adult supervision. The child's "street time" will increase. Street time is the amount of time that a child spends outside the home without adult supervision. More than eight hours a day in street time is a definite risk factor for potential trouble. More than likely, he/she is becoming overly involved in the subculture. We recommend that parents limit street time as much as possible. Two to three hours a day at this age is more than enough. It does not mean that the child has to spend all his or her time with the parent, but the parent will have to get actively involved in planning the child's time outside the home. We suggest that this is an excellent time to get the child involved in structured activities in the neighborhood. In a study conducted by the consultant group, Another View on Successful Off-Spring From Low-Income Single Parent Families, it was discovered that the parents of successful children planned many outside activities for their children. For example, in response to the question "What were the organizations, agencies, or institutions that contributed to your success? And why?" respondent Betty X said that her mother had chosen five organizations for her to attend. She hadn't realized it while it was happening, but her mother had just about planned all her outside activities and spare time. These activities were supervised by adults. She said that the supervising adults acted like her own mother.

Parents often believe that their children need them less during the latter years (8–13 years) of this stage. While it is true that older children are more independent, they still need their parents. If you have done your job well, they will brush and comb their hair, brush their teeth, wash up, and put on their clothes all by themselves. But you are still reminding them to do these things, and if you are still purchasing the soap, toothpaste, brushes, combs, and clothes, obviously they are not completely independent.

Parents also tend to decrease the quantity and quality of their involvement in their children's education. When children are in elementary school, parents are usually very involved. They are active in school organizations. They know their children's teachers and friends. They closely monitor their children's playmates during the early stages of Stage A. By the time a child enters the upper elementary grades, parents become less involved. They may only go to school for Parent Teacher conferences or Open House. At the high school level, African American parental involvement is even less—they almost disappear. This trend cannot continue if we are to make a positive impact on the subculture.

African American parents must prepare themselves for this period. Our children will try to make us believe we are clueless about what is going on in the world. Everything we did is "old school." "What do you know about what's going on today?" they'll say. In short, parents are not cool! Prepare yourself.

Parental Involvement by School Levels

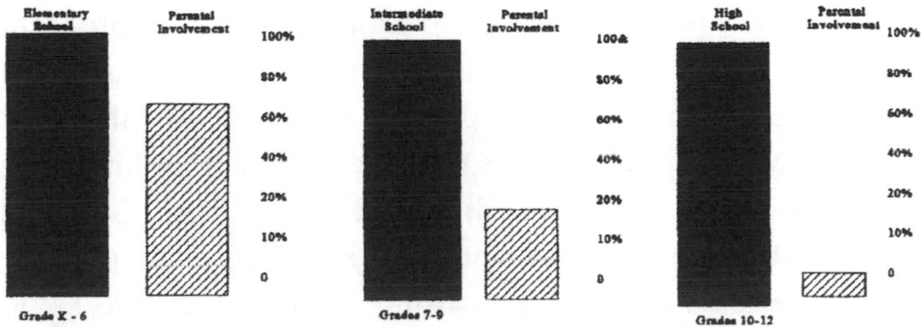

These results are based on 12 years of observation and working with African-American Families, who children attend the Cleveland Public School System.

We believe that some of the decreased involvement in our children's high school education is related to the fact that upper-grade schoolwork probably contains subjects with which parents are unfamiliar. Parents may not know how to help their children. Parents may be tired from working and grateful that the child is not bothering them. Whatever the reason, parental involvement decreases.

One example of the importance of parental involvement comes from the life of Malcolm X. One day Malcolm X told his teacher that he wanted to be a lawyer. He was an excellent student, president of his class, and well liked by his peers. His teacher informed him that his people made better carpenters than lawyers, and he should consider being a carpenter instead of a lawyer. We know the rest of the story. Would we have been reading a different story if Malcolm X's parent could have gotten involved? How many of our children today are being counseled to settle for less? Too many parents do not know because they are not involved in their children's education. African American parents, children need you, and you must be there for them.

The Breakfast Club Strategy

In an effort to increase parental involvement with adolescents, the authors helped to develop a prevention program called The Breakfast Club. This program was designed to prevent students from being suspended from school for a first offense. Most of the students referred to this program by the principals were from intermediate and high schools. Students and parents were given the option of attending this program, which was held on Saturday mornings from 8:00 a.m. to 12:00 noon at a community center. Refreshments were provided by the local McDonald's at no cost. Participants had to agree to fulfill certain conditions.

1. Both parent and child had to attend the Saturday morning session. (There were times when a childcare worker would attend with a child who was in custody of the county.)
2. All participants had to be on time and remain for the entire program.
3. All parents had to attend the parenting group.
4. All youth had to attend the youth group.
5. If the student violated the rules, he or she would be suspended.
6. A student could only be referred to The Breakfast Club once during the school year.

The Center also made their after-school, evening, and adult programs available to all the participants.

Allen Huff reports: One of my major responsibilities was to facilitate a parenting group. Mills's major responsibility was to facilitate the youth group. I would begin the group by discussing parental involvement in school and parenting skills. Parents would then give their reasons for their lack of involvement. The following are some of the reasons they shared:

- Timing of parenting meeting did not fit their schedule.
- School personnel were unfriendly.
- Entrance doors to the school were locked.
- Child care was unavailable for the younger children in the home.
- They were tired.

Then we would all discuss possible ways to remove the barriers. I followed up with the following questions:

Question 1
How many parents want their children to live with them for the next ten years?
Usually no hands went up.

Question 2
How many parents know what their children plan to do once they finish school?
Maybe one hand would go up.

Question 3
How many parents spend at least eight hours a week with their child?
Only a few hands would go up.

Question 4
If you believed that by investing eight hours a week with your child now you would guarantee that your son or daughter would not be living with you in the next ten years, would you do it?
Every hand in the house would go up. And this would start our discussion.

Every parent in the room wanted to know what to do to guarantee that their children would not be living with them in the next ten years. We explained that there were no guarantees, but there are things that parents could do to help their children be successful, such as:

- Spend time with them.
- Take an interest in what they are doing and what they plan to do.
- Set some limits for them.
- Provide them with direction and affection.

From these discussions, we would begin to map out times, dates, and places that would center around parent and child interactions. We let parents know that no matter how much their children resisted, they needed their involvement in their lives.

Albert Cobbs, the principal of the high school and a co-facilitator of the parents' group, presented the parents with a very simple but effective way of getting involved with their children's education. He presented them with the idea of making "pop calls" to the schools.

Pop calls are unannounced school visits. He told them that all they needed to do was to drop in at school at their leisure, walk the hallways, and/or sit in and observe the child's classroom. He said that as soon as the parent enters the door, someone would get the word to the child that his/her parent was in the school. Pop calls would do two things:

1. Monitor the child's behavior. Most children do not misbehave when their parents are in the building.
2. Monitor the child's academic performance. Teachers tend to take more interest in students whose parents come to the school.

Suspension rates at participating schools decreased. In addition, several important spin-offs occurred. More parents joined school-community councils, the principals joined the

Board of Trustees of community centers, and Pop Call Clubs were started that still exist today. More parents are actively participating in planning school activities for their children. The intermediate school that was involved in this project is a model school for the city of Cleveland.

African American parents of children at Stage A must provide direct contact and guidance to ensure they have the primary survival skills needed to adapt to their environment.

As the child grows into Developmental Stage B, the parent or caretaker is seen as the sunshine on the tree. In Stage B, the child's age ranges from 14 to 19 years old, and while the parent may no longer always have direct contact with the child, the parent must remain as a vital part of the child's growth and development. The sunshine symbolizes contact not always visible to our children, while its presence is always felt and very vital. And like plants that bend toward the sunlight, the parent wants the child to bend to their direction and guidance.

In the book *Climbing Jacob's Ladder: The Enduring Legacy of African-American Families*, author Dr. Andrew Billingsley writes the following about late adolescence:

> The late adolescent years between fifteen and nineteen are the most challenging. Like most parents, African-American parents face keeping their teens in clothes, food, and school. The challenge is most severe for low-income families. If parents have been successful in instilling a set of personal values about bodily care and correct conduct, adolescents will have a stronger set of armor with which

to fight the efforts of the peer groups, the street, and the mass media to reduce their appetites and conduct to the lowest common denominator. If families have nurtured a set of skills and high aspirations, they will have even more protection.[10]

Stage B is also called late adolescence. This is a period when the parent or caretaker must give the child more independence to bloom and grow, but the parent is still a powerful and needed element in the child's life. The African American parent will always remain the primary role model, but the parent may also actively seek secondary role models for the child.

Where do African American parents find these secondary role models, especially in these days and times when so much negative adult behavior is being directed at our children? In addition to relying on the extended family, the following are usually positive places where role models can be found:

1. Churches
2. Mosques
3. Schools
4. Community centers
5. Civic organizations
6. African American organizations
7. Political organizations
8. Businesses

One way for parents to find appropriate role models is to ask the child what he/she plans to do once school is completed. If he wants to be a carpenter, find a carpenter, or at least someone in the building trade, who has the time to mentor. One of our most challenging career pairings occurred when a young lady indicated that she wanted to become a stock broker. Where were we going to find an African American female stockbroker? Fortunately, we found one at a local brokerage house in Cleveland. Why do we tell this story? We tell it because so many times we do not believe such individuals exist or might be willing to participate in these types of programs. But have you asked them?

Role models must be carefully selected. They must espouse to the child the morals, beliefs, and values of the parents. These role models should be able to provide your child with information and positive experiences that will assist him or her in developing true substance.

Parents build self-confidence, courage, and independence in their children by allowing them to make informed choices. Children will be exposed to movies, cultural events, school and church trips, dances, and much more, but the parent firmly monitors the safety and appropriateness of all these secondary exposures. The parent will continue to push high expectations in education and complement the education with career awareness and career explorations. The child will benefit, the family will benefit, and ultimately, the African American community will benefit.

It is during this stage of adolescence that we have observed parents drastically pulling back, setting up safe distances, and communicating less with their children. Some additional reasons for this shift are as follows:

1. The child is not getting in trouble. If it isn't broken, why fix it?

2. Both parents are working or one parent is working two jobs, trying to make ends meet.
3. The child has concerns about issues, such as sexuality, which parents did not resolve as children, or even today as adults.
4. The child appears more independent and does not engage in conversation with parents.
5. The parents themselves are more concerned with style than substance.

We could argue the merits of these reasons for less involvement, but that is not important. What is important is that African American parents must seek help to make themselves better parents and to equip their children with the necessary armor to confront this world.

At this stage, parents should continue to have very in-depth discussions on human sexuality and hygiene. Discussions should explore the following topics:

- dating
- opposite-sex visitation to the home
- sexual intercourse
- love
- birth control
- sexually transmitted diseases
- positive and negative peer pressure
- marriage
- dress
- success
- respect for self

- respect for others
- personal hygiene

Parents must express their values, beliefs, and expectations about these issues. We always remind parents that if they do not initiate these discussions with their children, there is always someone in the streets who will. At this period of development, children have many questions and concerns about their own sexuality. Teens may be afraid or not know how to ask a parent, so parents must try to anticipate the child's questions.

Parents must be actively involved by instilling self-pride in their children. This can be done by teaching them about their rich culture and extensive history. Parents can no longer allow mass media, schools, and ill-informed individuals to miseducate our children.

African American parents need to understand and share with their children their rich African and American history. If the parents do not know about this history, this is an excellent opportunity for parents and children to learn together. Parents must seek out information which clearly proves that African American history did not begin with slavery. It began on the continent of Africa and flourished for centuries with kingdoms, empires, universities, and major cities.

Public schools would have children look at the pyramids and say that they came from outer space. They teach the "Great White Man" theory, having our children believing that only Whites can do anything. Parents need to understand and share with their children that many African Americans, in spite of slavery, rose to become great scientists and inventors. They accomplished these things because they were great, and so are we!

Stage B is also the time when children begin to look at themselves and examine how the rest of the world views them. Beauty standards become very important. Features such as hair color and texture, nose shape and size, hip size, and skin complexion will be closely scrutinized. They will be bombarded with phrases such as "good hair" and "pretty eyes." Most of our African American children will not fit the European standard of beauty. It is important for our children to understand that the issue of beauty is political and economic. If European physical features are considered "correct," then everything else is "incorrect." That means it must be "fixed." This, of course, costs money. African American parents, your job will be to communicate to your children the reasons for Europeans' features, African features, Asian features, etc. But, most importantly, your children must know that there is no "correct" skin color, hair texture, or nose shape. Beauty, as it is said, is in the eyes of the beholder.

When I (Allen Huff) was a boy, every morning before I would leave the house my mother would say, "You know, I have some beautiful Black children." She said this to us before it was fashionable or politically correct to use the word "Black." Her blessing helped me get through the day because I knew that if my mother said it, it had to be right. This also helped me ignore attempts by my peers and others to upset me by calling me Black. Her blessing helped to build my self-esteem. It helped make me the person I am today. I have continued this practice with my own children, grandchildren, nieces, and nephews, as well as the children I have worked with over the years. Parents, try it, you will be delighted with the response.

My mother also would tell us how much she loved us,

and because she loved us, she knew that we would not embarrass her under any circumstances. I continue this practice today with my own children as well as with all the young folks with whom I have worked.

This loving statement, "I have some beautiful Black children," did not take much of my mother's time, nor did it cost her any money to tell me that I was beautiful. But it certainly prepared me to deal with the world as well as myself. Every day I left her house knowing that someone loved me. I was ready to deal with the world.

Early on in this book, it was stated that African American parents must also teach their children about finances. We are recommending that parents discuss more than just how to balance a checkbook and secure a loan. These discussions should center around the economic development of the African American community. George Subira, in his *Black Folks' Guide to Business Success*, outlines 20 specific reasons why Black business is imperative to Black people's survival and development. In addition to teaching their children, parents should organize workshops on using credit and using ATM cards. Workshops on creating healthy attitudes and practices which lead to supporting Black businesses should be developed as well. Our children must understand that there is a proper way to complete an application form and dress for an interview. In addition, they must also understand that one day they can be the interviewer, not always the interviewee filling out the application for employment and interviewing for a job. Role-play if necessary. At this stage, parents must focus on teaching their children survival skills which allow them to move back and forth easily between White and Black America.

Lastly, the parents must give persistent and forceful direction to their children because of the tremendous amount of time they spend in the present-time thought zone. Mother Love states in her book *Listen Up Girlfriends!* "Yeah, love your kids with everything you got; but be tough with them because the world is a very tough place."[11]

Can African American parents alone provide everything that their children need to make it through these developmental stages and become successful? Probably not, but Black parents have the power to move both institutions and individuals. We recommend that Black parents use as many formal and informal helping systems as possible to assist in the rearing of their children. We must redefine family beyond the European nuclear definition of father, mother, and children. An African definition includes extended, nuclear, and single. All three models should utilize the resources of the larger community.

Attitudes toward Money and Work

One of the strongest influences in the formation of this African American subculture is the reaction to the information it receives about money. Most African American teens receive no special information about money from their parents other than the fact that money is extremely important for both survival and luxury. Parents convey the importance of money by working away their precious time. It is ironic that except for 118 vacation days and weekend days per year, most people spend 247 days per year in pursuit of money. This pursuit equals a grand total of 1976 hours annually of time spent on one goal, and the only thing money can't buy is time. The time computation does not take into account the person who has two jobs or a job and a half. Not only do most of us spend all our time making money, but we will move for it, marry for it, change for it, degrade ourselves for it, and go against our honor and moral principles for it. Some of us will cross greater boundaries for money than anyone can imagine.

What great power does money have? The power man has given it. In the introduction to *Creative Money Making*, Carly Llewellyn Wescheke states,

> Money of itself is a very magical force. Every dollar or pound you have in your possession right now is the condensation of some combination of three things—human labor, human skill, and material treasure. With money you can buy these things and you can sell these things for money.[12]

Given the great power and importance that we have assigned to money, we must discuss it in great depth with African American teens. African American teens already understand that money is important because they have given it almost as many names as Eskimos have given snow: greenbacks, snaps, duckies, dead presidents, greens, cabbage, ends, scratch, cheese, and dough, to name just a few. As parents we must discuss what money is and how it can be obtained within the family's moral code of conduct. We should discuss the importance of work and those things necessary to plan for a career or starting a business. We must teach our teens how to get a part-time job and how to dress and conduct oneself in a job interview. Discuss what you, as a parent, do for a living and your work ethic. Make it clear to your child that there are certain behaviors that will not be tolerated, such as selling drugs and dropping out of school.

Community

We African American adults must stop being afraid of our children. We must stop making excuses for our children's inadequacies and poor academic performance. We must demand respect from our children, and above all, we must give them respect. The African American community needs to demonstrate to our children that we can and will protect them as well as reward them for jobs well done. In short, we must begin to control our community.

There is a school of thought that states that environment affects behavioral outcome, thus the saying, "He or she is a product of his or her environment." It is our belief that individuals are not the sum of their experiences, but the sum of their *reactions* to experiences or environment. We are not products of our environment, but reactions to our environment. Clearly, an individual's perception of and reaction to experiences or environment is a key factor in the formation of a subculture.

Many immigrants in the 1920s gangster subculture experienced discrimination and reacted negatively to those experiences to acquire the desired results. African American teens are reacting to a lack of forceful adult direction and their own fear of the future. There is no greater paralyzer than fear. It is the emotion that is the catalyst for so many other negative reactions, such as racism, hatred, and anger. In Black communities, we adults fear our teens and the parents who allow their negative behavior. Black communities must rally together to enforce a strict code of behavior. African American teens are very perceptive. They can determine where certain types of behavior are allowed and also where they are not allowed. In most big cities, people know which communities allow drugs to be bought and sold without much resistance.

Black communities must resist teens' negative behaviors openly, strongly, and persistently. We as a community must pressure parents, police, and elected officials into enforcing the community's code of behavior. We must unify our communities and set behavioral standards for our teens. We must not fear them, because they are our children, and we are the adults. They will respect us for enforcing order; after all, every gang has rules of conduct and methods of enforcement. We must not allow some of the behaviors to continue. As a music group once stated in a song lyric, "Just what we permit, we allow."

As we stated earlier, we are not products of our environment or the sum of our experiences, we are the sum of our reactions to our environment or experiences. If we adhere to this trend of thought, then we must, as a community, adjust our environment so that positive reactions are increased. This effect can be accomplished by taking a good, long, thorough, critical look at our communities. If we insist on children becoming educated, Black communities must demand that money be spent on libraries and schools. Schools and libraries must expand their hours of service to the community, and the community, in turn, must utilize them. The entire atmosphere of the city and the local community must reflect the importance of education. Somehow, Black communities must provide quality education, and Black citizens must expect children to achieve academic success.

In most communities where African American teens exhibit destructive behaviors, funding can be acquired for midnight basketball before money is gained for schools and libraries. As a result, many African American males dream of becoming sports stars, but they do not earn the grades to get them near a college. Such social spending for prevention and intervention rather than education sends a clear signal to African American teens regarding what is truly important.

The most recent local example of this negative signaling to African American youth is the Save the Cleveland Browns Campaign, lead by Mayor Michael White. In the middle of the 1995 football season, the Cleveland Browns owner announced that he would be moving the team to Baltimore where he had obtained a financial incentive package that included a brand-new stadium. The mayor of Cleveland, who is a graduate of the public school system there and an African American male, spearheaded the Save Our Browns Campaign. The campaign became an all-out aggressive effort through radio, television, newspapers, petitions, and lobbying in Washington to keep the football team in the city. At the end, a deal was cut with the NFL and the Browns' owner. The city could keep the Browns' name and colors, and Cleveland would acquire a new expansion team in 1999 if the city would agree to build a new stadium. The city government, led by the Mayor, resolved to build a new stadium at a cost of $220 million, to be paid mostly through tax dollars.

Meanwhile, in the same city and almost simultaneously, the public school system was in state receivership because of its deficit of millions of dollars. Children did not have adequate school supplies, and schools were being closed because they were badly in need of repair. The same week that the city government announced its acceptance of the stadium deal, the school superintendent announced sweeping cuts in teacher personnel. A grand total of 73,000 students would be affected by these cuts, but there was no Save the Schools Campaign, no petitions, no media frenzy, no deals, and certainly no tax dollars. A few local parents tried to attract city government's attention, but without success.

As a result of the city's decision to emphasize the importance of sports to the community via voter and monetary support, 50 percent of Cleveland's high school students did not report to school to take the state's ninth-grade proficiency test. Schools had urged parents to take a pledge of responsibility "for their children's education," and the police conducted truancy sweeps; yet high school students responded by refusing to attend. Why? Children are perceptive enough to know the difference between what adults say and what adults mean. We can no longer blame our state of affairs solely on politicians. They are supposed to represent their constituencies' desires and wishes. If they do not, we have the power to remove them from office. Our politicians must help us create the community atmosphere to which our young people will react positively. The atmosphere that we want to create must reflect safety, morality, and education. We are sure we do not want to raise our families in neighborhoods that are dirty, fragmented, drug infested, beverage store littered, and crime ridden.

Community control is alive and healthy outside of the nation's largest cities. The African American community must begin to ask why it is failing at community control. Then we must take action to reclaim control of our communities. As Mills likes to quote, "Our youth are out of control because what we permit as a community, we allow as a community."

Take education, for example. African American communities need to create an atmosphere where education is a priority and does not take a backseat to sports and entertainment. We must put to rest the current myth in the younger generation's minds that the only way an African American can make it out of the ghetto is on an athletic scholarship. We must not only speak about education, but we must spend our money on education. We must set up learning centers and libraries in our homes. We must promote reading and learning in our neighborhoods and form community groups promoting education. Our Black communities must reward academic achievements. Above all, we must create the atmosphere in our communities that encourages learning.

The following example illustrates how we created this atmosphere at an intermediate school in Cleveland, Ohio. The following activities were planned around pupil induction into the National Junior Honor Society. To be inducted into the Society, a pupil had to maintain a minimum 3.2 grade point average and have excellent behavioral marks.

National Junior Honor Society induction ceremonies are usually planned by a teacher, who is the advisor to the group, and a committee of teachers. This particular Honor Society

Induction Committee included students who had been inducted previously, the advisor, the principal of the school, several community leaders, parents, and staff from the community center. Students indicated that they wanted the ceremony to be upbeat with music, just like the sports rallies. One student wanted to know why only certain students were invited and why the rest of the student body was excluded. All the students agreed that they did not want a boring speaker. The community leaders wanted to know if they could make special proclamations. The parents wanted the program to be at a time when they did not have to rush out to get back to their other children. Everybody had specific concerns, and we tried to take all of them into consideration.

This is what finally took place: The principal made provisions for the entire student body to attend the assembly. Originally, he was apprehensive because of the student-to-teacher ratio. He was concerned about what would happen if a behavioral problem occurred. Parents and community center staff agreed to act as chaperones, which solved the student-to-teacher ratio problem. There were no problems.

A speaker was invited. He spoke on what the inductees as well as the entire student body had to offer the world. He used several examples that the students were familiar with to explain his points. And the most important aspect of his speech was that he spoke in a language that they understood. The students gave him a standing ovation.

The band and cheerleaders from Central State University, a historically Black college located in Wilberforce, Ohio, were invited to perform. The band members and cheerleaders played several routines, and several other types of music (rap and jazz) were played prior to and following the ceremony. When the honorees' names were called, each one stepped through a paper ring. The students received special recognition the whole day. They had special seats in the cafeteria. Their lunches were free. Their names were posted on the school bulletin boards. The principal also made sure that refreshments were available for all the adults who attended. A special reception was held for these students whose pictures were taken with their parents, community leaders, and school personnel. Overall, the students were made to feel special for their accomplishments. Today, this school has been designated as one of the model schools in the city of Cleveland, and their National Junior Honor Society continues to grow.

Style mentality has created an atmosphere in our communities in which failure and negative behavior are rewarded. What do we mean? We mean that African American teens no longer ridicule their peers if they underachieve in academics; instead, they will ridicule their peers for overachievement in academics. Our observations revealed the following typical example: Smart children are referred to as "nerds," "geeks," "brainiacks," "robots," "computer heads," etc. Smart children are ostracized from teen social functions, such as parties, dates, and dances. On the other hand, underachievers are not ridiculed at all, and most of the time they are very popular in the teen social scene. What we permit, we allow. This type of behavior can no longer be tolerated in or by the African American community.

Even more, our communities must be cleansed of crime. We must not fear our children, and if they have gone astray and are acting in inappropriate ways, they must understand that they will meet swift and forceful consequences for their actions. We must protect our children who act appropriately from their out-of-control peers. Our neighborhoods belong to us, and we must no longer turn our backs on criminal activity.

The African American community needs to know that Black Americans make up 13 percent of the general population, but in virtually all spheres—offenders, victims, prisoners, and arrests by the police—the rates for Blacks are disproportionate to their share of the population. Thus, Black men account for 51 percent of those incarcerated. They also comprise 40.1 percent of the prisoners currently under sentence of death. Overall, more than a million Black Americans are currently behind bars or could be returned there for violating probation or parole.

Black youth must understand that this country has no qualms about locking them up. According to the Federal Judicial Center, the average sentence for Black people on weapons and drug charges were 49 percent longer than those for Whites who had committed and been convicted of the same crime. And the disparity has been rising over time. Indeed, it is also most important for the community to know these statistics, so that it may become "scared straight" and "get its act together." The Black community must begin to demand and assist with the design of programs and policies to prevent the assault on our youth from continuing. When one of us commits a crime and it goes to trial, we are all on trial. We must stand up and deal with the problem.

Our children want control, leadership, and rules, because if they didn't, they wouldn't join gangs. Gangs have street rules, leadership, control, and a swift and direct way to deal with any infractions. Gangs also provide protection from other teens who invade their space and break their rules. Our community must be as strong as any of the African American youth gangs, and if we are not, we, as a people in the United States will perish. We must protect our teens and make our homes, communities, and schools safe. We must not fear our teens. After all, we gave them life. They will never respect us if we fear them.

We African Americans must demand help from our elected officials to help change the atmosphere of our communities, or they must go. We cannot vote for them on the basis of color, popularity, religion, or what they did twenty years ago. Votes must be cast based on what they are doing and can do for the community now. It is time for the community and elected officials to present and work from a united front. In the book, *Torchlight For America*, the Honorable Minister Louis Farrakhan says:

> Black organizations and leadership must focus on self help. . . . Each Black organization and every Black leader has a role in the upliftment of our people. We must recognize and respect each other's

role and learn to work with those with whom we may be at variance ideologically. We should consider establishing a united front for the purposes of converging our efforts to meet common objectives over one, three, five and ten years.[13]

Black elected officials can play a crucial role by forming powerful coalitions with other political forces to

1. Promote education as a priority.
2. Sponsor legislation to create crime-prevention programs for teens.
3. Sponsor legislation that will create a living wage for all age groups.
4. Create fair-trade agreements.
5. Create quality education in our public school systems.

The African American community must also increase its involvement in the political arena. No longer can it be assumed that the Black community will automatically vote Democratic. To be a political force, we must do the following:

1. Promote and organize leadership-training workshops.
2. Promote and organize voter-registration drives.
3. Promote and organize voter-education campaigns.
4. Promote and organize "Get Out to Vote" campaigns.
5. Promote and organize candidates and issue nights.
6. Endorse candidates and issues.

7. Recall candidates.
8. Monitor candidates' voting and legislation records.
9. Attend hearings on local, state, and federal levels.

In short, the African American community must become politically active. We can no longer be taken for granted, and we can no longer be ignored. We must become a political force. Our youth should be involved in all phases of these activities because it will demonstrate that they have a stake in what goes on in the Black community. Such participation will build their substance.

A new mentality needs to be adopted by the African American community as it relates to employment. The last time there was full employment for the African American community was during slavery. Do we want full employment? Yes! Do we want slavery? No! Nor should the African American community want slave or minimum wages. We should be demanding guaranteed full employment at a living wage for every able-bodied person in our community. As a community, we should support businesses and political leadership that promote this as a part of their agendas and practice it in their operations.

African American teens need placement in jobs that will train them. We should demand that the numerous businesses that operate in our communities hire and train them. We must make it clear to these businesses, by any means necessary, that if they wish to operate in the Black communities and make a profit, they must have a commitment to hiring our people.

The community must begin to teach our youth early on in their development that it is not impossible to own and operate their own businesses. The community must prepare our youth to deal in the global economy, not just the street economy. Economic development is not just for other cultures; we must commit to developing our neighborhoods through education, economic planning, and implementation. Through economic empowerment, the African American community can step forward to neutralize this negative style subculture and render it another footnote in our history.

What can African American community-based organizations do to make a positive impact on the negative teen subculture? Community-based organizations must begin to conduct critical analyses of their programs. As Carter G. Woodson said in *The Miseducation of the Negro*:

> The program for the uplift of the Negro in this country must be based upon a scientific study of the Negro from within to develop in him the power to do for himself, what his oppressors will never do to elevate him to the level of others.[14]

A significant number of community-based organizations administer programs that operate from "Deficit Model." The Deficit Model is founded on the negative behaviors and characteristics of a small number of the youth population, programs such as teen pregnancy programs, restitution programs for juvenile delinquents, or juvenile first-offender programs. They are designed to track and prevent negative behavior rather than promote positive behavior.

Community-based organizations should begin to concentrate more of their efforts toward prevention. Prevention programs are culturally based and focus on resolving the normal developmental issues of the youth and their families. These programs are founded on the strengths of the people they are trying to assist, not the weaknesses. Such programs would target larger segments of the Black teen population. Prevention programs assist African American families who are struggling to keep their children focused on their future goals.

Community-based organizations should begin to design programs such as the Positive Education Program. This was designed and implemented by the co-authors, and it is presently being implemented in several community organizations based in Cleveland, Ohio. The program was designed with input from program participants—youth, parents, and community leaders.

The Positive Education Program was designed for students in grades one through twelve. Its focus is family preservation. It was imperative that the organization develop a mission statement that was inclusive of and rooted in African culture. African culture is centered around family preservation. This statement was finally agreed upon:

This mission requires the provider to operate from a "Strength Model" and not a "Deficit Model." According to the Strength Model, service providers must assist an individual or individuals based on their capacities and abilities to develop solutions and strategies to deal with their areas of concerns.

The staff members of community-based organizations need to develop a new mind set and understand that the community is their major partner in solving the problems that exist in the African American community. If service providers were able to realize the power in combining the resources of our profession with that of the community, as a people, we would be invincible.

To support the mission of family preservation, the Positive Education Program builds on the following program components:

1. History and culture
2. Human sexuality
3. Exposure
4. Personal development
5. System changes
6. Goal setting

The Positive Educational Program encourages participants to place historical dates, places, people, and events within an African American frame of reference. The Program teaches students that they are making history, and what happens tomorrow will depend on them.

The first group was composed of those participants who

were referred by Juvenile Court or resided in the community in 1987. The program was administered through a community-based agency and was staffed with social-service providers. In adapting the program to the specific realities of students in their communities, providers had to identify the age range of participants to be served as well as choose developmentally appropriate material and activities. The program lasts for twenty weeks: students in grades one through six attend four sessions per week; grades seven through twelve attend two days per week.

The following core topics are covered in the weekly sessions:

1. Personal Development
    a. Sense of identity
    b. Peer group association
    c. Values clarification
    d. Survival skills
2. Goal Setting
    a. Responsibilities
    b. Education
    c. Personal/family
    d. Ten-year plan
3. History and Culture
    a. What is history and culture?
    b. Unity/Umoja
    c. Making history
    d. The Nguzo Saba

4. Human Sexuality
    a. Making choices
    b. Dating
    c. Respect
    d. Hygiene
    e. Feelings
5. System Change
    a. Economic Development
    b. Education
    c. Justice
    d. Family

Youth are referred to this program by probation officers, teachers, parents, school personnel, ministers, and street clubs. Some just walk in with their friends. The groups are open and the only requirements to join are that the youth arrive on time.

The topics are covered in the order given above. Before each topic is introduced to the groups, a general assembly is held with all groups to discuss the agenda for the upcoming month. After each topic is completed, a celebration is held. Parents attend and the participants make presentations. The presentations reflect lessons learned from each topic. It is perfectly okay if presentations overlap, but presentations must include information from the topic. Separate celebrations are held for the elementary and junior/senior high school groups. However, both groups come together to celebrate following the completion of the History and Culture section.

Leading the groups requires training and preparation. To educate a group leader with some of the issues facing our African American youth and the African American community in general, we strongly recommend that leaders read. We also use relevant and up-to-date media, including movies, videos, records, radio, television, and cable programs which portray positive African American values. African American experts can also be invited to provide additional training to staff. There is nothing worse than an uninformed group leader who chooses not to use the resources at his or her disposal to get the job done. Group leaders should attend conferences and workshops such as those hosted by the National Association of Black Social Workers and the National Black Child Development Institute to stay abreast of issues and solutions.

There must be creativity in our approach. Before the 20-week program begins, leaders should visit the homes of as many prospective group members as possible. They need to get to know the families. It's also important and helpful to visit homes after the program has begun. Attendance at participants' extracurricular activities is crucial, and encouragement of parental involvement is important. Group workers need to attend local African-centered cultural and educational events.

A critical element of the program is the exposure of participants to a variety of cultural and educational experiences. As the saying goes, "the more you see, the more you know you can be." African American children suffer from closed minds and limited vision. Expand a Black child's horizons, and you create an African American person with unlimited potential. Youth workers are responsible for planning field trips to vocational schools as well as colleges. Both white-collar and blue-collar workers are needed in the ongoing struggle for African American survival.

As with any program, annual evaluation is critical to program success. Constant feedback from all the participants should be used to improve the program. Thus, it is important to maintain appropriate and accurate information. Staff should continue to add to the reading list and meet at least once a week to discuss their successes and failures. The program works best as a team project. When one person is successful, all will benefit. It should also be recognized that while most social workers have been taught to focus on the negative, this program calls for rethinking traditional approaches. It necessitates learning to identify and build on the strengths of Black youth. This is crucial, and although it might be hard, it must be done.

All meeting rooms are decorated in an African American motif. Such a setting helps teens feel good about themselves, enhances their appreciation of their culture, and overall enriches the learning environment.

After the program has been implemented for five months, junior and senior groups are broken down into special interest groups. These groups can be co-ed and are held together for three months. The special interest groups should include, but are not limited to, the following participants:

1. Seniors, college bound
2. Non-seniors, college bound
3. Seniors, vocational and trades
4. Non-seniors, vocational and trades

College-bound seniors should work on the following:

1. Improving GPA and college placement test scores
2. Securing college applications
3. Visiting colleges
4. Completing financial aid forms

College-bound non-seniors (seventh, eighth, ninth and tenth graders) should work on:

1. Deciding which high school courses to take
2. Visiting colleges
3. Planning for college
4. Applying for financial aid
5. Choosing a college based on their interests and goals

The vocational and trades seniors should work on:

1. Apprenticeship programs
2. Military programs
3. Visiting trade and vocational schools
4. Applying for financial aid

The vocational and trades non-seniors should work on:

1. Summer job placement in their areas of interest
2. Job forecasting
3. Visiting trade and vocational schools
4. Military programs

The Program also encourages participants to consider entrepreneurship as an available strategy for economic survival and development.

Evaluation

Many worthwhile community-based programs fail to use evaluation tools to measure the progress of their participants and the success of their programs. Inevitably, this omission adversely affects the ability of organizations to evaluate their effectiveness. It also hurts chances of obtaining additional funding.

The following High Risk Scale evaluational tool was developed by the authors and implemented in several community-based organizations in the City of Cleveland. This instrument measures the potential for success as well as the potential for failure. One of the major features about this instrument is that parents, teachers, community workers, ministers, and other service providers can be taught to use it.

HIGH RISK SCALE

NAME___________________ AGE____ GRADE_____

SCHOOL________________

A. FAMILY HISTORY

B. WHO WOULD YOU LIKE TO BE AND WHY?

1. STREET TIME
2. SCHOOL ACADEMIC PERFORMANCE
3. SCHOOL BEHAVIOR
4. SCHOOL ATTENDANCE AND TARDINESS
5. PEER GROUP ASSOCIATION
6. ASPIRATION
7. PARENTAL/GUARDIAN INVOLVEMENT
8. SIBLING PAST HISTORY
9. ALCOHOL AND DRUG INVOLVEMENT
10. SELF-ESTEEM

HOW TO USE AND UNDERSTAND THE HIGH RISK SCALE

1. *Street Time*—the amount of time that an individual spends away from home in an unsupervised setting. (e.g., hanging out with peers.) Clearly, time spent at school, church, a recreational center, etc., does not apply. We believe that if street time equals more than

eight hours a day, Monday through Friday, the student is at risk.

2. *School Academic Performance*—the grade point average received on the most recent report card. A significant drop (such as from A to C or C to F) needs special attention.

3. *School Behavior*—indicated on report cards. In elementary school, students are checked on their ability to follow rules and respect property. At the junior high and senior high level, attitude marks are usually indicated. Students with unsatisfactory attitude marks are at risk, regardless of their grades. For example, a student who has eight courses and has five unsatisfactory marks and three satisfactory marks is at risk.

4. *School Attendance and Tardiness*—indicated on report cards. It is indicated by stating the days absent and tardy. Any student who has more than seven unexcused absences or tardinesses in any marking period is at risk.

5. *Peer Group Association*—The question is not "Who are your friends?" but "What do you and your friends do when you all get together in an unsupervised adult setting?" Any anti-social behavior indicates a student at risk: drinking, cutting classes, doing nothing, driving other people's cars, stealing, and so forth.

6. *Aspirations*—what an individual aspires to become. Special attention should be paid to the role of education and how it is related to a plan to achieve their aspirations. An individual who has no aspirations is at risk. An individual who has unrealistic goals is also at risk.

7. *Parental/Guardian Involvement*—the amount of time spent with a parent or guardian in some meaningful exchange, e.g., eating dinner, going to church, discussing homework, or just sitting down talking. Lack of adult involvement indicates a child at risk.

8. *Sibling Past History*—To provide a more complete family picture it is important to understand the student's relationship to siblings. What are the academic, social, employment, and religious experiences of siblings, and how have they affected the student's outlook? If there is a family history of anti-social behaviors, the student is at risk.

9. *Alcohol and Drug Involvement*—If there is a suspicion of alcohol and drug use, the student is at risk.

10. *Self-esteem*—If a child can feel good about himself, even if he doesn't have much or even if he is involved in anti-social behavior, this is good. If a child feels as though he doesn't have much to offer himself or the world, this is an indicator of high risk.

Each of these categories has specific implications for counseling approaches.

At the end of the interview, the test administrator must allow time for the youth to express herself or himself. He records the interview in the child's words. Each question must be answered. There are no right and wrong answers. If a child says he doesn't know the answer, he/she is encouraged to answer by paraphrasing the question so that it can be understood. It is the child's answers that are important, not what the recorder thinks is said.

Organization Evaluation

It is important to critically analyze how the organization delivers services. The areas that we recommend for organizations to consider are as follows:

1. *Leadership Development.* Is there a set of designed activities to assist individuals and families within the community to assume leadership roles?

2. *Sustainability.* Is there the ability to ensure continuity of effort and relationships with families and communities?

3. *Inclusivity.* Is there a recognition of the differences that exist among community residents and the valuing of these differences as reflected in agency policy and practice in your organization?

4. *Shared Responsibility/Accountability*. Is there a mutual understanding and implicit contract between neighborhood organizations and families which promote and preserve the well-being of families and the neighborhood?

5. *Neighborhood Priorities*. Is there a process which makes it possible for programs to respond to neighborhood and family needs and issues?

6. *Collaborative Relationships*. Are there active strategies that provide communication, joint activities, and shared vision between and among agencies, neighborhood groups, and families?

7. *Spirituality*. Is there a set of beliefs and values that contributes to a sense of meaning and hope for an individual, family, and community well-being?

8. *Accessibility*. Are there processes, attitudes, and structures within the organization that support full and equal participation by all who are part of the community?

9. *Neighborhood Governance*. Are there ongoing decision-making and oversight conducted by neighborhood residents?

10. *Capacity Building*. Are there strategies and opportunities which enable families, neighborhoods, and agencies to acquire and maintain the essential psychological, physical, and economic resources for growth and development that build capacity?

We highly recommend the tool kit which provides hands-on strategies that are designed to ensure that a program is effectively meeting the needs of young Black people and their families.

Community-based organizations must become *more* user-friendly to all teens. Currently, there are few structured activities that cater to teen needs. For example, the midnight basketball program is great for getting drug dealers off the street, but what about the "good" teens who don't get into trouble? There are many. Community-based organizations can no longer neglect to create programing for this population.

Community-based organizations must begin to reconsider their hours of operations. Are the hours more convenient for the staff, or are the hours convenient for the teen population they serve? In our travels around the country, we have noticed that many organizations serving youth close early during the week and are not opened at all on the weekends! Clearly we are missing golden opportunities to reach our target population. Evenings and weekends are excellent times to plan trips, invite role models to speak, host career nights, and plan special programs like an Academic Dinner Dance, for instance.

The African American teen subculture described in this manuscript did not develop because our youth are innately irresponsible, helpless, and directionless. It developed because we African American adults in the community did not recognize their cries for help. They need us and we need them. Let us begin to do our job. A strong child makes a strong adult. A strong adult makes a strong family. Strong families make a strong community. Strong communities make strong nations. "It's nation building time."

[1]Norma Freeman and Don Freeman, "Authentic Community: The Crucible for People of African Descent in the United States of America," *Vibrations* 2 (4): 7 (1995).

[2]Marlene Kim Connor, *What Is Cool?: Understanding Black Manhood in America* (New York: Crown Publishing Group, 1995), p. 119.

[3]Veronica Webb, The Forbidden Word, Section C1, *The Plain Dealer*, Cleveland, Sunday, 12/4/96.

[4]Florence Schovel-Shinn, *The Power of the Spoken Word* (Marina del Rey, CA: Shinn Press, 1945).

[5]Naim Akbar, Ph.D., *Chains and Images of Psychological Slavery* (Jersey City, NJ: New Mind Productions, 1984), p. 1.

[6]Webster *New Riverside Dictionary*, Houghton-Mifflin (1998).

[7]Sultan A. Latif and Naimah Latif, *Slavery: The African-American Psychic Trauma* (Chicago: Latif Communication Group, 1994), p. 276.

[8]Sultan A. Latif and Naimah Latif, *Slavery: The African-American Psychic Trauma* (Chicago: Latif Communication Group, 1994), p. 279.

[9]Marquits Hill, *Training African-American Parents for Success, An Afrocentric Parenting Guide* (Cleveland: East End Neighborhood House, 1992), pp. 6-7.

[10]Andrew Billingsley, Ph.D., *Climbing Jacob's Ladder: The Enduring Legacy of African-American Families* (New York: Simon & Schuster, 1992), p. 61.

[11]Mother Love with Connie Church, *Listen Up Girlfriends!* (New York: St. Martin's Press, 1995), p. 185.

[12]Denning and Phillips, *Creative Money Making, Become a Money Magnet* (St. Paul, Minnesota: Llewellyn Publications, 1992), p. xiii.

[13]Minister Louis Farrakhan, *A Torchlight for America* (Chicago: FCN Publishing, 1993), p. 40.

[14]Carter G. Woodson, *The Miseducation of the Negro* (New York: AMS Press, 1977), p. 144.